1. The gateway to Arno's Castle, with the colonade and Black Castle behind, connected to Arno's Court Mansion by a tunnel under the road. The name Arno is said to originate from a copy of one on the banks of the River Arno in Italy.

2. The Courtyard of the Black Castle built by William Reeve, from Black Slag from the waste from his copper smelter at Crews Hole. He built Arno's Court Mansion about 1760, and the Black Castle was used as his stables. This card was posted in 1916.

BRISLINGTON

The Tram Depot, Sandy Park, Brislington.

3. The Brislington Tram Depot, on the corner with Sandy Park Road. The tram on the main road to Brislington Village, about to ascend Kensington Hill. Card postally used in 1911.

Bristol Tramways Illuminated Car December - 1924

4. One of many decorated trams which collected funds each Christmas in the 1920s, for the Lord Mayors' Christmas Appeal. This view inside the tram depot in 1924.

5. Kensington Hill, a wide thoroughfare, with large Victorian double bay villas. This view shows early telegraph poles, and the curve of the tram line to enter the depot.

6. Arno's Vale Mansion became a convent about 1851, and it was the first Roman Catholic Reformatory in England, as many as 200 girls were accommodated. A Chapel was added in the Victorian period. This card was posted in 1911.

Kensington Hill, Brislington.

7. Another view of Kensington Hill looking towards Brislington Village. Card postally used in May 1912.

8. The top of Kensington Hill with no pavement on the left, looking back down the hill. This postcard was posted in May 1912.

9. Hampstead Road. A long road which runs from Kings Road, and crossing Kensington Park Road, connects with Talbot Road. This view about 1910.

10. Kensington Park Road towards Knowle. Only fields lie between the end of the road and the Roman Catholic Church on the hill, with the water tower just visible behind.

11. Sandy Park Road from the bridge over the former Bristol and North Somerset Railway, taken over by the Great Western Railway in 1884, Butts Stores on the corner with Repton Road. The lodge of Wick House in Wick Road facing down from the top of Sandy Park Road. Card postally used in May 1913.

12. Sandy Park Road in the opposite direction from picture No.11, A.A. Comer's Post Office and Store on the corner of Winchester Road. There were several brothers and relations who published views of Brislington.

13. The Crescent, houses on the main Bath road. The shop and Post Office on the corner of Winchester Road owned by Comer & Co. The postcard published by A.E. Comer, Brislington.

14. A different angle of the Crescent, with tram no. 213 enroute to Hotwells from Brislington Village. The postcard was posted in April 1923, and published locally by J.B. Comer.

15. The corner of the Crescent, with Wick Road and the Brislington United Reform Church on the opposite corner. Postcard published by LT. Elson of Sandy Park Road, and posted in March 1924.

16. A closer view of the United Reform Church, looking along Grove Park. The house at the far end is known as Grove Hall. It was owned for many years by the Ricketts family, who were major partners in the Pheonix Flint Glass Works in Portwall Lane in Temple Gate, and lived at Grove Hall until around 1900. Card postally used in November 1911.

17. The Church Hall at the top of Bristol Hill, on the main road to Bath. A horse trough and water fountain in the centre of the road.

18. West Town Bridge, children relaxing in the sun for the photographer, the stream running under the bridge flows into Water Lane adjoining West Town Lane Farm.

19. Water Lane. The railings on the edge of the stream can be seen in illustration 18. Could the children be the same group? A shaded view looking along Water Lane.

20. Water Lane completely flooded, with two delightful young girls standing on the higher piece of ground by a wooden gate, before 1914.

21. "The Golden Shred" works at Brislington, an aerial view showed the extent of the works in its rural setting, situated adjoining Brislington Station.

22. The staff of the "Golden Shred" factory posing in a group for the photographer outside the offices of the works seen in illustration 21. Postcard published by H.M. Veale of Bristol.

Front View. Golden Shred Works, Brislington. 1889.

23. Robertson "Golden Shred" works in 1915, with fields between the factory and the Knowle Water Tower, which was built in 1905. The Jam factory closed down in 1980.

RAILWAY STATION, BRISLINGTON

24. Brislington Railway Station opened in September 1873, on the Bristol and North Somerset Railway Line to Radstock, and was then operated by the G.W.R. from 1884. It was closed in October 1959 to passenger traffic, and goods traffic in October 1963.

25. Bristol Hill with tram no. 223, descending into Brislington Village, the tower of Brislington Church in the distance. Postcard published by L.T. Elson of Sandy Park Road, and posted in 1924.

26. A closer look at Brislington Village from the open ground opposite the large houses on Bristol Hill. Postcard published by A.E. Comer.

27. The Kings Arms Inn, one of the oldest surviving Inns in Brislington. The old forge can be seen to the left of the tram, with the bridge over the stream leading to the square. This view published by Lillywhite of Sowerby Bridge, Yorkshire.

28. Looking in the opposite direction from the bridge in Brislington. Rogers Pale Ale's advertised on the wall of the forge. The house (Wisteria House) was demolished in 1939.

29. By the wall of the Kings Arms Inn, looking along Grove Road, now known as Hollywood Road, a man standing beside the open door of the forge.

30. Another view by the bridge looking towards Wisteria House, the shop advertising Fry's Pure Cocoa, with Ye Olde Village Tea Room sign on the wall.

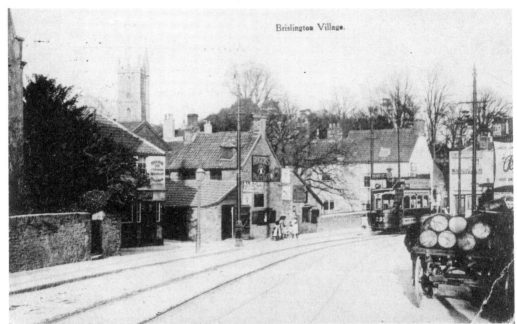

31. Amongst one of the earliest views of this part of Brislington on a postcard, as it was posted in October 1906. The Parish Church of St. Lukes on the left, and the cottage behind the tram faces the square.

32. The vicarage, a charming old house, has a commanding position overlooking Brislington and in the direction of the Parish Church.

BRISLINGTON

HIGH STREET, BRISLINGTON   Foster, B'ton

33. Another very early postcard, posted in December 1904, the forge with a cart horse being shod and behind the cart Brislington Post Office. Opposite the tram the house called Homeside, Mr. A. Skilling and his family lived there between 1907-1928.

The Square, Brislington.

34. The Square, Brislington, showing the post office with two shops adjoining. Many adverts on the walls, including Brooks Dry Cleaners, Colmans Starch and Lyons Tea. The Wesleyan Chapel on the end, opposite "Woodlands" the large house in Church Row.

35. Across the square from the Post Office. A group of men probably reading the latest news in either the Bristol Daily Mercury, or Bristol Echo. These papers advertised on the hoardings near them. This picture before 1909, as the Mercury Newspaper ceased publication before then.

36. School Road by the junction with Granton Close. The school was destroyed in an air raid in world war II, and the cottages on the right are now demolished. Only the School House adjoining the church remains today.

37. This view shows the open ground on the left opposite the school. Postcard published by F.J. West of Brislington Post Office, who was also the local under-taker. His sign is seen in illustrations 34 and 35. Postally used in 1927.

38. School Road, with children walking in the road in 1922. Recognisable today, but the cottages on the left have been demolished. Published in the Chatterton Series by A.G.S. & Co., Bristol. Postally used in July 1922.

BRISLINGTON

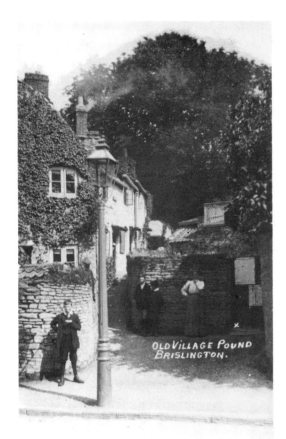

39. The village pound, situated at the bottom of Brislington Hill, between Brislington Post Office and the house called Homeside. The walled area by the cottages housed stray animals before 1914, and survived to the 1930s.

40. Talbot Lane, a narrow thoroughfare when this postcard was published by Harvey Barton of Bristol, is now known as Talbot Road. It connects with Brislington at the one way system at the top of Bristol Hill, and at Priory Road, Knowle. This postcard was postally used in 1916.

BRISLINGTON

Bristol Hill from West Town Lane
Brislington.

41. The view from West Town Lane when fields stretched to Bristol Hill, Kenneth Road and Warrington Road are two of the main connecting roads now built there. Postcard published by L.T. Elson.

Old Brislington.

42. A delightful group of children in the field near Hollywood Road. The old village of Brislington behind, with the school with its pointed spire on the left, and the church amongst the trees.

43. A snow-bound distant view of old Brislington, with houses spread around the church. Postcard written and posted on 23rd June 1911.

44. Grove Park Avenue, a turning off of Montrose Avenue, behind the Brislington United Reform Church, and Grove Park.

45. Montrose Avenue is a turning off of Wick Road and connects with Fry's Alley, in the direction of Brislington church. The shop on the corner was owned by W.H. Smith, an advert for Cadbury's Chocolate can be seen on the wall. Posted March 3rd 1914.

46. Churchill Road, a turning off Bloomfield Road, behind Brislington Tram Depot. This view about 1910 shows many children, and a delivery man with his basket.

47. Sandgate Road, one of the main roads off of Sandy Park Road, with 'Sand' in their name. It connects Sandhurst Road with Sandringham Road.

48. Sandgate Road in the opposite direction to illustration 47. Both postcards published by J.C. Young.

49. Winchester Road, a turning in from Kensington Hill on the main road. Shops include a chemist and confectioner. Note the children in their summer hats! Postcard postally used in September 1911.

50. Another view of Winchester Road showing the double bay villas with decorated wooden eaves and a horse and cart delivering Pale A.K. Ales.

51. Winchester Road with one of the many corner shops, yet another postcard published by J.B. Comer.

52. Harrow Road originally in "New" Brislington, when the houses were first built in the area. It joins with Sandy Park Road and Winchester Avenue.

53. Wick Road Council Schools, a group of mothers with prams and children outside the entrance to the Infant School. Postcard published in the York series.

54. Wick Road, the turning for Trelawney Park on the left, with the wall and railings of the Council School Opposite. Postcard posted in August 1926.

55. Wick House, in Wick Road, was built in the late 1790s. It had extensive grounds and was owned for a time by Thomas Harding, Paint Manufacturer, about 1881. The property was bought by the Church of England Society, who opened it as a home for waifs and strays in 1924.

56. The bottom of Brislington Hill, with the road curving around the tree, and many advertising hoardings beyond. The house with the large yew trees is Linton Farm which supplied milk to the Brislington area.

Brislington Tram Terminus and White Hart Hotel.

57. The tram terminus at the bottom of Brislington Hill, with a tram waiting. The White Hart Hotel on the left, with double gates beyond, advertising 'Good Stabling'. Postcard published by N.J. West, undertaker, residence, post office, Brislington.

58. Looking in the opposite direction to illustration 57. The White Hart Hotel, a coaching inn, on the Bristol-Bath Road, was built about 1738. Postcard published by Lillywhite of Sowerby Bridge.

Brislington Hill Garden.

59. Brislington Hill House, situated near the top of Brislington Hill, built about 1798 by Mr John Hurle. The family took the name Cooke-Hurle through a later marriage.

Brislington Hill Garden.

60. The extensive gardens and greenhouses with St. Lukes church between the trees. Before the war the house was converted into flats, after being sold to Mr George Gay. The house was badly damaged in an air raid during the 1939-45 war, and was later demolished.

61. The lodge of Brislington Hill House at the top of White Hart Hill, also known as Brislington Hill. This was the entrance to the former Cooke-Hurle family home, and was removed for road widening in 1966. Card posted in May 1910.

62. This cottage is situated between Brislington and Keynsham looking North East towards Stockwood Farm. The postcard was posted in February 1914.

63. Birchwood Road connects Brislington with St. Anne's, from Allison Road to Guildford Road. Postcard published by Senior & Co., Cotham Hill, Bristol, and postally used in October 1914.

64. Eastwood Road. A turning off of Birchwood Road with its large houses and varied architecture. Another postcard published by Senior & Co., Cotham Hill about 1914.

65. First Avenue before 1910, at the bottom of the road, Station Road leading to St. Anne's Park Station. Postcard published by Senior & Co.

66. First Avenue in about 1940, looking in the opposite direction of illustration 65. Published locally by D.G. Parker, 4 Birchwood Road, St. Anne's.

67. Langton Court Road, a turning off of Newbridge Road. J.H. Rea, Newsagent and Tobacconist on the corner, with adverts for Reckett's Blue and Zebra Grate Polish above the doorway. An unusual view, as it was photographed on a wet day.

68. Langton Court Hotel was built on the site of Langton Court House which was demolished about 1900. This postcard was published by Coe of the Post Office, Brislington, not long after the hotel was built.

69. The Post Office in Langton Court Road, on the corner with Maple Road. An early postcard, when St. Anne's was known as New Brislington. Posted in October 1905.

70. Addison Road has been renamed and it is now Highworth Road. It joins with Newbridge Road, and Arlington Road. Another postcard by E. Coe in 1918.

Addison Road, New Brislington.

71. Addison Road (now Highworth Road), a very early view. Postcard posted in February 1906.

ARLINGTON RD. ST ANN'S.

72. Arlington Road, a turning off the beginning of Newbridge Road, not far from New Brislington Bridge, and extending to Langton Court Road. Postcard postally used in February 1918. The I.C.I. chimney stack, pointing skywards, was demolished in 1947.

ST. ANNE'S

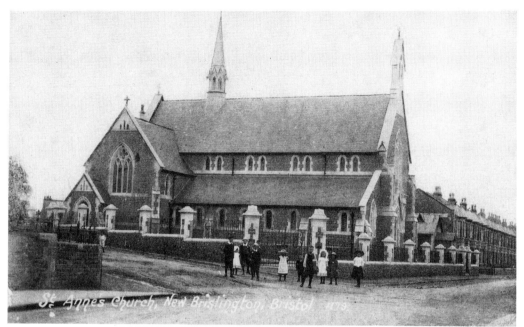

73. St. Anne's church on the corner with Salisbury Road and Langton Road. The original Iron Church, built in 1903, can be seen between the present church and the houses adjoining. The postcard was published by Harding of Bristol and Cardiff, and posted in September 1905.

74. The Schools, St. Anne's. The Primary School on the corner of Langton Court Road and Bloomfield Road, built before 1902. Children gathered in front of the school for the photographer.

75. Salisbury Road, with the east window of St. Anne's church on the left. St. Anne's Primary School at the end of the road. The neat double bay villas, with a rather stoney road. This view postally used on November 8th 1910.

76. Newbridge Road. These houses face St. Anne's Park, at the end nearest St. Anne's Station. Postcard posted on September 20th 1918.

Newbridge Road, New Brislington.

77. Newbridge Road. An early view in April 1907, when the area was known as New Brislington. The shop, St. Anne's Supply, run by W. Comerford. The hoarding advertising the Castle Bazaar, held at Arno's Castle.

THE WOODS. ST ANNE'S

78. The woods, St. Anne's. A summers day with a young man in his straw boater hat strolling along the path. Another postcard published by E. Coe, and posted from Bristol August 11th 1918.

79. Three Pools. St. Anne's wood with the park keeper, and children looking in the direction of the photographer. Photo by Hepworth.

158. St. Anne's Well. Brislington.

80. St. Anne's Well, a Holy place in the woods. Picture published by Avonvale, before 1914. F.C. Jones was successful in getting the well covered in 1929. A Chapel was founded in the wood, before 1392 by De La Warr. A place of pilgrimage, it came to an end when Henry VIII dissolved the monasteries.

ST. ANNE'S

81. St. Anne's Park Station. The church of St. Anne's on the skyline, the cottages in Nightingale Valley overlooking the station. This picture postcard posted August 1912. The station opened on 23rd May 1898, and closed on 5th January 1970.

82. The Great Western Steam Engine "King Harold" just entering St. Anne's Park Station. Postcard published by W. Vaughan-Jenkins, Combe Down, Bath.

ST. ANNE'S

A Peep at St. Anne's Station.

Photo. Winchester.

83. St. Anne's Station from Nightingale Valley, with the large houses of First Avenue on the hill. The station was on the Bristol to Paddington Great Western Line. Postally used January 1909.

Nightingale Valley, St. Anne's Park.

Photo. Winchester.

84. Nightingale Valley, the cottages also known as St. Anne's Terrace, in a very rural setting overlooking the station. Photo by Winchester, the postcard posted on January 1st 1912.

Estate Office, St. Anne's Park.

85. The Estate Office belonging to the Sinnott Family. Two unmarried sisters named Emery bred horses on a farm at one time. The Estate Office still survives today, in a much wider and developed Birchwood Road. Postcard posted from Saltford on August 15th 1908.

BEESE'S TEA GARDENS. ST ANNE'S .10.

86. Beese's Tea Gardens on the banks of the River Avon, with rowing boats moored. The gardens were owned by Mr Plumton and many boats called there on river trips, as well as by ferry from St. George, or through nearby Eastwood Road.

INDEX